Pineapple-Rice Pudding ....

Apple-cinnamon rice pudding ....

Blueberries Breakfastquinoa ....

Savory lentils 8

Cranberry Green Cabbage Quinoa 9

Creamy coconut rice 10

Creamy carrot risotto 11

Curry leaf rice 12

Steamer maize cobs 13

Steam cooked sweet potatoes 14

Steamed Green Beans 15

Steamed mussels with black bean sauce 16

Steamed butternut pumpkin 17

Dijon chicken with Farro and mushrooms 18

Simple Vegetarian Penne 19

Simple couscous 20

Simple Edamam ice cream 21

Plain Spanish Rice 22

Plain wild rice 23

Plain oatmeal quinoa 24

Simple Garlic Quinoa 25

Simple Quinoa 26

Peas-corn rice 27

Fresh berry blend compote 28

Fresh asparagus with tofu 29

Frittata with summer vegetables	30
Fruit Beans Quinoasalat	31
Fruit magic with quinoa salad	32
Steamed Rice Beans Chili	33
Turmeric Curry Quinoa	34
Mixed vegetables quinoa	35
Healthy quinoa salad	36
Pomegranate Pears Magic	37
Pomegranate-Mint Quinoasalat	38
Pomegranate Quinoa Salad	39
Green Beans Quinoa	40
Green cabbage lentil dish	41
Curly kale raisins quinoa	42
Hot vegetable cake	43
Jalapeno bread	44
Jamaica Rice	45
Classical hummus	46
Small barley magic	47
Garlic-Lemon Rice	48
Coriander rice	49
Coriander-Lemon Rice	50
Mushroom rice with cabbage and green beans	51
Salmon potato gratin	52
Prepare tasty corn dip	53
Tasty Basmati rice	54

Delicious coconut rice	55
Delicious Mexican rice	56
Tasty risotto	57
Tomato Beans Quinoa	58
Lenses Quinoa	59
Corn cabbage Quinoa	60
Corn-Olive-Carrot-Pea Quinoa	61
Sea rice magic	62
Midnight omelette	63
Delicious mussel mix	64
Orange marmalade	65
Orange-Rice Plov	66
Pancetta with green cabbage and spaghetti pumpkin	67
Pasta Carbonara	68
Peppermint truffle	69
Mushroom rice Plov	70
Pinto beans rice cooker type	71
Polenta with cheese	72
Quiche from the rice cooker	73
Quinoa broccoli casserole	74
Quinoa vegetables Plov	75
Quinoa with juicy apple	76
Smoked salmon fritatta	77
Brussel sprouts with walnut oil	78
Rosemary chicken	79

Red Quinoa with rice	80
San Antonio rice	81
Hot cheese dip	82
Sharp lentil rice	83
Fast rice cooker paste	84
Fast chicken curry	85
Fast Quinoa-Porridge	86
Swiss rice cake	87
Prepare homemade kimchi	88
Shrimps with Grits	89
Shrimps with lemon risotto	90
Asparagus with tofu	91
Spinach, chickpea and green cabbage Quinoa	92
Southern corn pudding	93
Sweet potatoes with rice	94
Sweet pudding	95
Thai rice	96
Vegetarian noodle soup	97
Vegetarian Curried Rice	98
Vegetarian Black Bean-Chili	99
Wheat sprout salad	100
Lemon Dill Rice	101
Lemongrass shrimp soup	102

4 servings - time required: 1 hour

Pineapple-Rice Pudding

Ingredients

350ml rice milk

300ml water

1 pinch of salt

170g jasmine rice

75g sugar

120g egg powder

1 tsp. vanilla extract

1 tin of pineapple in its own juice, chunky

Nutrient information per serving
309 Calories
10g Fat
34g Carbohydrates
5g Protein

- Add 200ml rice milk and water to the rice kettle.
- Cook with the "White rice" setting. The mixture may boil quietly.
- Add rice with salt. Allow to rest for at least 30 minutes. Activate the warming function.
- Whisk the remaining rice milk, egg powder, sugar and vanilla in a bowl.
- Add the pineapple and fruit juice.
- Add the mixture to the rice milk, which is still warm and cooked, and mix.
- Let it boil until everything becomes viscous.
- Done.

4 servings - time required: 40 minutes

Apple-cinnamon rice pudding

Ingredients
225g white rice
240g apple, cored and diced
1 tablespoon vanilla extract
60g vegan butter
420g Vegan condensed milk
1 pinch of nutmeg
150g raisins
750ml water
1 pinch of salt

Nutrient information per serving
468 Calories
12g Fat
85g Carbohydrates
5g Protein

- Put rice, apples, raisins, nutmeg and water in a rice kettle and mix well.
- Cooking.
- Add butter, vanilla and condensed milk after cooking. Mix well.
- Boil again until all liquid has been absorbed.
- Mix well and refine with cinnamon.
- Serve warm and enjoy.

4 servings - time required: 30 minutes

Blueberries Breakfastquinoa

Ingredients
170g Quinoa, rinsed and dried
100g blueberries
1 tsp cinnamon
A pinch of cinnamon
1 teaspoon nutmeg
2 tablespoons sugar
1 tsp. vanilla extract
500ml unsweetened almond milk

- Crush blueberries with a fork.
- Put all the ingredients in a rice cooker and stir well.
- Cook with "White rice" setting.
- Stir again and serve well.

Nutrient information per serving
484 Calories
31g Fat
46g Carbohydrates
9g Protein

2 servings - time expenditure: 40 minutes

Savory lentils

Ingredients
2 tablespoons extra virgin olive oil
1 pinch of curry powder
1 teaspoon caraway seeds
200g Brown lentils, washed
700ml water
1 tin of tomatoes, strained
1 small onion, diced
1 tablespoon dried vegetables
2 tbsp parsley, chopped
1 pinch of salt
1 pinch of pepper

Nutrient information per serving
276 Calories
14g Fat
23g Carbohydrates
6g Protein

- Add the ingredients to the rice cooker and mix well.
- Select the "White rice" setting and let it cook.
- Stir 1-2 times in between.
- Allow to cool for 10 minutes.
- Done.

1 serving - time required: 25 minutes

Cranberry Green Cabbage Quinoa

Ingredients
60g Quinoa, washed and dried
2 tablespoons orange juice
1 tablespoon olive oil
40g dry cranberries
35g green cabbage, minced
160ml water
A pinch of cinnamon
pepper
salt

Nutrient information per serving
381 Calories
17g Fat
47g Carbohydrates
9g Protein

- Put the quinoa, orange juice, olive oil, cranberries, green cabbage and water in a rice cooker. Mix well.
- Cook in a rice cooker for 20 minutes. Stir 2-3 times in between.
- When it boils, add cinnamon, pepper and salt. Mix well again.
- Serving.

8 servings - time expenditure: 50 minutes

Creamy coconut rice

Ingredients
900g Basmati rice

840ml coconut milk

1 touch of turmeric

1 pinch of cinnamon

1 pinch clove powder

1 pinch of caradamon powder

Nutrient information per serving
566 Calories
24g Fat
79g Carbohydrates
8g Protein

- Add the ingredients to the rice cooker and mix well.
- Let it boil.
- Stir well after cooking.
- Serve warm.

4 servings - time required: 40 minutes

Creamy carrot risotto

Ingredients
225g arborio rice

750ml vegetable stock

1 onion, diced

2 carrots, sliced and peeled

1 tablespoon olive oil

15g vegan butter

Nutrient information per serving
254 Calories
8g Fat
43g Carbohydrates
3g Protein

- Heat butter and oil in the rice cooker.
- When the oil is hot, add onions and carrots.
- Cook for 5 minutes.
- Add the rest of the ingredients and mix well.
- 30min cooking.
- Mix and serve.

4 servings - time required: 30 minutes

Curry leaf rice

Ingredients
450g white rice

20 curry leaves

180ml coconut milk

360ml water

1 pinch of salt

- Add the ingredients to the rice cooker and mix well.
- Cook with "White rice" setting.
- Mix the rice with the fork and serve.

Nutrient information per serving
435 Calories
10g Fat
76g Carbohydrates
7g Protein

1 serving - time required: 15 minutes

Steamer maize cobs

Ingredients
400ml water

Corn cobs, halved

- Place the corn on the top of the steam cooker.
- Put water in rice kettle.
- Steam cook for 10 minutes.
- Done.

Nutrient information per serving
174 Calories
5g Fat
22g Carbohydrates
13g Protein

1-2 servings - time required: 25 minutes

Steam cooked sweet potatoes

Ingredients
500ml water

500g sweet potatoes

- Peel and dice the potatoes.
- Add water to the rice cooker.
- Steam cooked for 17 minutes.

Nutrient information per serving
231 Calories
5g Fat
21g Carbohydrates
11g Protein

2 servings - time required: 15 minutes

Steamed Green Beans

Ingredients
500ml water

500g Green Beans

- Put water in rice kettle.
- Place the green stages in the top of the steamer and let it cook for 10-12 minutes.

Nutrient information per serving
44 Calories
0g Fat
10g Carbohydrates
3g Protein

1 serving - time required: 20 minutes

Steamed mussels with black bean sauce

Ingredients
500g mussels, cleaned
500ml water
2 tbsp water
1 teaspoon brown sugar
3 cloves of garlic, ground
2 spring onions, finely chopped
4 tablespoons paprika powder
Half a teaspoon of fish stock
15g Coriander, chopped

Nutrient information per serving
347 Calories
11g Fat
24g Carbohydrates
31g Protein

- Add water to the rice kettle and heat.
- When it boils, add the mussels and cook for about 6-8 minutes.
- Cook the mussels until they are all open.
- Place finished mussels on a plate.
- Prepare black bean sauce with 2 tsp water and other ingredients. Sauté the ingredients in a pan for 1-2 minutes.
- Add to the mussels.
- Done.

2 servings - time required: 15 minutes

Steamed butternut pumpkin

Ingredients
500g butternut, peeled and diced

500ml water

- Put water into the rice cooker.
- Place the pumpkin on the steam cooker top.
- Cook for 10-12 minutes.

Nutrient information per serving
82 Calories
0g Fat
22g Carbohydrates
2g Protein

2 servings - time required: 1 hour 30 minutes

Dijon chicken with Farro and mushrooms

Ingredients
150g chicken breast fillet
1 teaspoon olive oil
2 spring onions, diced
240g Crimson mushrooms
120g Farro
360ml vegetable stock
Half a bunch of parsley

Marinade:
80ml balsamic vinegar
1 teaspoon extra virgin olive oil
1 tbsp. Dijon mustard
1 pinch of salt and pepper

Nutrient information per serving
435 Calories
6g Fat
25g Carbohydrates
31g Protein

- Prepare marinade and marinate chicken.
- Cook olive oil and spring onions for 5 minutes with standard settings.
- Add the mushrooms and cook for another 8 minutes.
- Add Farro and cook for 3 minutes.
- Add the broth and the chicken, which has now been marinated. DO NOT add excess marinade.
- Add parsley as well.
- Let it boil for an hour.
- Done.

4 servings - time required: 25 minutes

Simple Vegetarian Penne

Ingredients
300g wholemeal noodles
1 tin of white beans
1 tin of tomatoes, strained
1 tin of tomatoes, lumpy-sharp
75g sweet onion, diced
350g Broccoli, crushed
1 tablespoon ground garlic
100g radishes, halved
500ml vegetable stock
250ml water

Nutrient information per serving
207 Calories
3g Fat
32g Carbohydrates
7g Protein

- Mix the ingredients and cook with the white rice setting.
- Stir twice in the meantime.
- Done.

4 servings - time required: 30 minutes

Simple couscous

Ingredients
170g couscous

500ml vegetable stock

1 spring onion, chopped

1 tablespoon olive oil

Half a teaspoon of salt

Nutrient information per serving
221 Calories
4g Fat
36g Carbohydrates
8g Protein

- Put olive oil in a rice cooker and heat.
- When the oil is hot, add the spring onion and steam.
- Then add the couscous and cook for several minutes stirring constantly.
- Add vegetable stock and salt. Stir well. Let it continue to boil.
- Finally mix again and serve.

6 servings - time required: 40 minutes

Simple Edamam ice cream

Ingredients

450g white rice

360ml water

40g Edamame

1 tablespoon olive oil

1 clove of garlic, grinding

3 tablespoons white wine

A touch of pepper

A pinch of salt

Nutrient information per serving
268 Calories
3g Fat
50g Carbohydrates
5g Protein

- Put rice, water and white wine in a rice cooker and switch on the appliance.
- Boil Edamame for two minutes in boiling water and drain well.
- Heat the olive oil in a saucepan at medium heat.
- Add the garlic and fry for one minute in the pan. Then add Edamame and stir well.
- Season the edamame with salt and pepper.
- Add the rice, which has now been boiled, to the pot and mix well.
- Done.

4 servings - time required: 35 minutes

Plain Spanish Rice

Ingredients
340g rice

1 teaspoon caraway seeds

2 tablespoons olive oil

300g tomatoes, cut into pieces

360ml vegetable stock

Nutrient information per serving
342 Calories
8g Fat
58g Carbohydrates
7g Protein

- Add the ingredients to the rice and mix well.
- Close the rice cooker and cook for 30 minutes.
- Mix well as soon as ready and serve.

4 servings - time required: 50 minutes

Plain wild rice

Ingredients
225g wild rice

500ml vegetable stock

1 pinch of salt

- Spray rice cooker with cooking spray inside or drizzle with oil.
- Add wild rice, salt and vegetable stock. Mix well.
- Cook for 40 minutes.
- Then mix again well and serve.

Nutrient information per serving
162 Calories
1g Fat
30g Carbohydrates
8g Protein

6 servings - time required: 30 minutes

Plain oatmeal quinoa

Ingredients
100g oatmeal, ground

120ml almond milk

Half a teaspoon of cinnamon

800ml water

120g Bulgur, ready to cook

100g oatmeal, in flakes

Nutrient information per serving
131 Calories
2g Fat
24g Carbohydrates
5g Protein

- Put the oatmeal, bulgur, salt and water in a rice kettle and mix well.
- Let it boil until all the water is absorbed.
- Add almond milk and cinnamon.
- Optional: garnish the oatmeal mixture with yoghurt and serve.

4 servings - time required: 35 minutes

Simple Garlic Quinoa

Ingredients
340g Quinoa, rinsed and dried
75g onions, minced
1 teaspoon of chopped garlic
1 tablespoon olive oil
600ml vegetable stock

- Put the olives in a rice cooker and sweat them.
- Add the onion and garlic and fry for 3 minutes.
- Add Quinoa and stir for one minute.
- Add the vegetable stock and mix.
- Cook the quinoa mixture for 25 minutes.
- Mix well with a fork and serve.

Nutrient information per serving
373 Calories
9g Fat
56g Carbohydrates
15g Protein

4 servings - time required: 40 minutes

Simple Quinoa

Ingredients
170g Quinoa, washed and dried

420ml vegetable stock

Olive oil at will

A pinch of salt

- Add the ingredients to the rice and mix well.
- Boil the mixture until all the water is absorbed.
- Mix the quinoa well before serving - done.

Nutrient information per serving
172 Calories
3g Fat
27g Carbohydrates
8g Protein

4 servings - time required: 35 minutes

Peas-corn rice

Ingredients
225g rice

90g corn kernels

75g peas

75g onions, chopped

1 tsp paprika powder

2 tbsp parsley, chopped

360ml water

1 pinch of salt

Nutrient information per serving
208 Calories
1g Fat
45g Carbohydrates
5g Protein

- Sprinkle the rice cooker inside with cooking spray or cooking oil.
- Add the ingredients to the rice cooker and mix well.
- Cooking.
- After cooking, let it rest for 10 minutes in the holding mode.
- Mix the rice well with a fork and serve.

4 servings - time required: 30 minutes

Fresh berry blend compote

Ingredients

200g strawberries, halved

100g blueberries

125g raspberries

1 tablespoon lime juice

Half a teaspoon of vanilla extract

1 tbsp water

75g sugar

Nutrient information per serving
113 Calories
0,5g Fat
28g Carbohydrates
1g Protein

- Add the ingredients to the rice cooker and mix well.
- Close the rice cooker and boil.
- Once cooked, stir everything well again and serve.

4 servings - time required: 30 minutes

Fresh asparagus with tofu

Ingredients
180g firm tofu, diced
Half bunch of asparagus, peeled
1 teaspoon honey
1 teaspoon
1 dash of rice wine
1 teaspoon sesame oil
1 teaspoon vegetable oil
1 clove of garlic, minced
Half peeled carrot, chopped

Nutrient information per serving
65 Calories
4g Fat
4g Carbohydrates
4g Protein

- Mix all ingredients well in a large bowl.
- Put the mixture in a rice cooker.
- Stew for 25 minutes.
- Stir and serve.

2 servings - time required: 30 minutes

Frittata with summer vegetables

Ingredients
1 clove of garlic, peeled
1 onion, diced
1 potato, diced and diced
1 courgette, sliced
1 pinch of salt
1 pinch of pepper
1 tablespoon olive oil
1 tablespoon oil for the pan (according to preference)
6 eggs laid
2 tablespoons of grated cheese according to personal taste

Nutrient information per serving
177 Calories
12g Fat
10g Carbohydrates
8g Protein

- Heat the oil in a pan.
- Add the garlic clove until it turns brown. Then remove it.
- Add the vegetables. Season to taste with salt and pepper. Then remove the whole from the heat.
- Add olive oil to the rice cooker and drizzle it inside.
- Add all the ingredients and cook with normal settings. Stir well before use.
- Done.

8 servings - time required: 35 minutes

Fruit Beans Quinoa salad

Ingredients
190g Quinoa
500ml water
50ml orange juice
50ml lime juice
12 chopped jalapenopaprika
30g peppermint
30g coriander, chopped
1 red pepper
100g Black Beans, cooked and drained
100g avocado, chopped and peeled
330g mango, sliced
2 tablespoons balsamic vinegar
2 tablespoons olive oil
Half a teaspoon of salt
pepper

Nutrient information per serving
357 Calories
11g Fat
55g Carbohydrates
12g Protein

- Put the quinoa, water and salt in a rice cooker. Mix well and cook for 15min.
- After 15 minutes, pull the quinoa with a fork and put it into the mixing bowl.
- Mix vinegar and olive oil.
- Add the vinegar/olive oil mixture to the quinoa and stir well. Put aside for cooling.
- Once the quinoa is cold, add orange juice, lime juice, jalapenopaprika, peppermint, coriander, red pepper, black beans, avocado and mango. Mix well.
- Season the salad with salt and pepper.
- Serve and enjoy.

10 servings - time required: 30 minutes

Fruit magic with quinoa salad

Ingredients
340g Quinoa
A bunch of peppermint
95g pecan nut, roasted and crushed
1 peeled and sliced orange
1 peeled and chopped apple
550ml water
2 teaspoons of cinnamon
1 tablespoon maple syrup

Nutrient information per serving
211 Calories
7g Fat
34g Carbohydrates
6g Protein

- Put water and quinoa in a rice cooker.
- Cook with the brown rice setting.
- Once Quinoa is cooked, put it in a bowl.
- Pour the remaining ingredients into the bowl. Stir well.
- Ready to serve.

3 servings - time expenditure: 45 minutes

Steamed Rice Beans Chili

Ingredients
115g rice
1 teaspoon oregano
1 teaspoon cumin seed
1 pepperoni
1 teaspoon ginger
1 green peppers, chopped
1 clove of garlic, minced
Half an onion, chopped
250ml water
300g tomatoes, sliced
90g sweet corn
120g Black Beans

Nutrient information per serving
618 Calories
2g Fat
118g Carbohydrates
32g Protein

- Put tomatoes, onions, ginger, garlic and water in a rice kettle. Mix well.
- Select the quick cooking function. When it starts to boil, add the remaining ingredients.
- After 15 minutes of cooking, stir well once.
- Serve warm.

4 servings - time required: 30 minutes

Turmeric Curry Quinoa

Ingredients
170g Quinoa, washed and dried
200ml water
1 pinch of paprika powder
1 teaspoon turmeric
2 tbsp garlic powder
2 tablespoons dried parsley
2 tsp onion powder
300g tomatoes, chopped

- Put the ingredients in a rice cooker and cook until all the liquid has been absorbed.
- Stir well and serve.

Nutrient information per serving
196 Calories
3g Fat
36g Carbohydrates
7g Protein

4 servings - time required: 30 minutes

Mixed vegetables quinoa

Ingredients
170g Quinoa, washed and dried

2 tablespoons Amino liquid

1 tablespoon sesame oil

200g mixed vegetables of your choice

700ml vegetable stock

Nutrient information per serving
259 Calories
7g Fat
37g Carbohydrates
12g Protein

- Put vegetable stock and quinoa in a rice cooker. Stir everything well.
- Place the vegetables on top of the steamer. Place it over the quinoa.
- Cook the quinoa with the white rice setting for 20 minutes.
- Then put the vegetables and quinoa into a large bowl.
- Add the amino liquid and sesame oil. Mix well.
- Serve warm.

6 servings - time required: 40 minutes

Healthy quinoa salad

Ingredients
Lettuce:
8.5g Quinoa, rinsed and dried
200ml water
2.5g vegetarian cheese, grated
7.5g cherry tomatoes, sliced
60g cranberries, dried
7.5g cucumbers, sliced
7.5g peas
Dressing:
1 vol. spring onions
1 tablespoon lime juice
1 lemon zest
1 tablespoon vinegar
2 tablespoons olive oil
1 pinch of pepper

Nutrient information per serving
125 Calories
6g Fat
18g Carbohydrates
3g Protein

- Put water and quinoa in a rice cooker and boil it with a pressure cooker.
- In the meantime, mix the dressing ingredients in a bowl.
- Once the quinoa is cooked, stir it well with a fork and put it in a bowl. Allow to cool for 5 minutes.
- Add tomatoes, cranberries, cucumber, peas and cheese.
- Add the dressing and mix well.
- Serve and enjoy at once.

2 servings - time required: 2 hours or the day before

Pomegranate Pears Magic

Ingredients
2 pears, halved
500ml pomegranate juice
500ml apple sparkling wine
1 stick of cinnamon
1 Clementine bowl, grated
2 cloves of garlic
2 aniseed stars
3 Cardamom Capsules
1 piece of ginger, chopped
orange cream sauce

Nutrient information per serving
252 Calories
6g Fat
43g Carbohydrates
6g Protein

- Put the ingredients in a rice cooker. Cook for 50 minutes with the white rice setting and the lid closed.
- Open and turn the bulb halves.
- Leave the food in the rice cooker for one hour.
- After another hour, turn the bulb halves over again.
- Store in a cool place overnight.
- Serve garnished with orange cream sauce.

8 servings - time expenditure: 30 minutes

Pomegranate-Mint Quinoa salad

Ingredients
340g Quinoa, rinsed and dried
15g peppermint, chopped
Half a teaspoon of spice mixture
150g pomegranate seeds
1l water
1 tablespoon olive oil
2 tbsp. lime juice
35g roasted pine nuts
1 pinch of salt

Nutrient information per serving
216 Calories
7g Fat
28g Carbohydrates
7g Protein

- Put the quinoa, salt and water in the rice cooker and mix well.
- Cook with "White rice" setting.
- After cooking, mix the quinoa with a fork and put it in a bowl.
- Add lime juice and spice mixture - mix again.
- Finally, add the remaining ingredients and stir thoroughly.
- Serving.

4 servings - time required: 30 minutes

Pomegranate Quinoa Salad

Ingredients
340g Quinoa
1l water
1 pinch of salt
170g pomegranate seeds
Half a teaspoon of spice mixture
15g peppermint, chopped
35g roasted pine nuts
2 tablespoons lemon juice
1 tablespoon olive oil
1 pinch of pepper

Nutrient information per serving
163 Calories
4g Fat
23g Carbohydrates
12g Protein

- Put the quinoa, salt and water in the rice cooker. Cooking.
- In the meantime (or already before) roast the pine nuts in a pan.
- After cooking, pour the rice mixture into a mixing bowl and add the spices and lemon juice.
- Allow to cool.
- Add the remaining ingredients and mix well.
- Serve and enjoy.

4 servings - time required: 30 minutes

Green Beans Quinoa

Ingredients
170g quinoa, rinsed and dried
350ml water
75g roasted cashew nuts
3 tablespoons vinegar sauce
1 tomato, unpicked and chopped
360g green beans, crushed and stalk base removed
1 teaspoon salt

Nutrient information per serving
341 Calories
16g Fat
40g Carbohydrates
10g Protein

- Put the quinoa, salt and water in a rice cooker. Stir well and cook with white rice.
- As soon as the quinoa boils, place the green beans on top of the quinoa.
- Cook the green beans for 5 minutes.
- Remove the beans with the steam cooker top and cook the quinoa for another 15 minutes.
- Mix the quinoa well with a fork and put it in a bowl.
- Add the chopped tomatoes, the green beans and vinegar sauce. Stir well.
- Spread cashews as decoration over the quinoa. Serving.

4 servings - time required: 45 minutes

Green cabbage lentil dish

Ingredients
200g Brown lentils

270g green cabbage, chopped

1 tbsp Italian herbal mixture

1 bay leaf

2 cloves of garlic, ground

120ml water

500ml vegetable stock

Nutrient information per serving
235 Calories
2g Fat
37g Carbohydrates
17g Protein

- Add the ingredients to the rice and mix well.
- Cook for 40 minutes with the brown rice setting.
- Mix and serve.

1 serving - time requirement: 30 minutes

Curly kale raisins quinoa

Ingredients
60g Quinoa, rinsed and dried
130g green cabbage, chopped
60ml almond milk
A pinch of cinnamon
3 tbsp raisins
180ml water
A pinch of salt

Nutrient information per serving
464 Calories
17g Fat
69g Carbohydrates
12g Protein

- Put the quinoa, water, salt, cinnamon and raisins in the rice cooker. Mix well.
- Cook in the cooker. As soon as the unit switches to the keep warm mode, open the lid and mix again.
- Add kale and almond milk. Stir well and leave to stand for 5 minutes in the keep warm mode.
- Serve and enjoy.

1 serving - time required: 15 minutes + optional pancake baking

Hot vegetable cake

Ingredients
1 egg
120ml milk
15g carrots, cut and peeled
50g pumpkin, diced and pre-cooked
75g spinach, chopped
1 pancake mixture
(1 serving = 2 slices)

- Mix the ingredients together and place in a rice cooker.
- Cook for 5-10 minutes in the oven, depending on your personal taste.
- Serving.

Nutrient information per serving
272 Calories
4g Fat
23g Carbohydrates
13g Protein

3 servings - time required: 35 minutes

Jalapeno bread

Ingredients
320g flour
1 teaspoon yeast
1,5 tbsp. sugar
1,5 tsp. salt
1 teaspoon salt
25g butter
2 tablespoons milk
200ml water
80g sliced jalapeno (hot peppers)
75g cheddar, grated

Nutrient information per serving
75 Calories
1g Fat
2g Carbohydrates
1g Protein

- Add yeast with sugar and 60ml warm water in a bowl.
- Let it rest for ten minutes (should foam by itself).
- Add flour and salt to the rice cooker and mix.
- Add the milk and yeast mixture to the rice cooker as well. Mix well.
- Put butter in the middle of the dough. Jalapeno's on top, over the butter.
- Cook in a rice cooker.
- Serving.

4 servings - time required: 45 minutes

Jamaica Rice

Ingredients
225g white rice
1 teaspoon Jamaican jerk spice mix
500ml vegetable stock
60g red pepper, diced
50g raisins
20g roasted coconut flakes
150g sweet potato, chopped
2 spring onions, chopped
2 tsp. ginger, grated
1 clove of ground garlic
1 sprig thyme
50g ground coriander, ground

Nutrient information per serving
290 Calories
3g Fat
57g Carbohydrates
7g Protein

- Add the ingredients to the rice and mix well.
- Cooking.
- Mix the prepared rice with a fork and serve.

2 servings - time expenditure: 12-24 hours or 40min working time

Classical hummus

Ingredients
200g chickpeas
1 tbsp. tahinapaste
3 tablespoons olive oil
1 teaspoon cumin, ground
1 tsp coriander, ground
2 cloves of garlic
60ml lemon juice
1 pinch of salt and pepper

Nutrient information per serving
223 Calories
7g Fat
24g Carbohydrates
30g Protein

- Let the chickpeas simmer overnight in 1.5 litres of water.
- Rinse the chickpeas and put them in the rice cooker.
- Cover with water, so that the surface of the water is about 2cm above the chickpeas.
- Cook with "White rice" setting.
- Mix the chickpeas and other ingredients with a mixer or food processor.
- Done.

2 servings - time required: 2 hours

Small barley magic

Ingredients
500ml water
200g barley
2 sticks of celery, finely chopped
1 onion, diced
4 cloves of garlic
4 slices of bacon, cooked and minced
2 sprigs of thyme
60g cranberries
70g bread (or croutons)
2 eggs
250ml chicken stock
2 tbsp/30g butter

Nutrient information per serving
149 Calories
1g Fat
32g Carbohydrates
5g Protein

- Add the barley and water to the rice pan.
- Cook with the brown rice setting.
- When the cooking process is over, add bacon, celery, onion and garlic. Cook for 5 minutes.
- Add bread and butter. Distribute the butter as well as possible on the bottom.
- Select the cake function (alternatively: 1.5h normal cooking function), add the remaining ingredients and mix well. Close the lid and bake or boil.
- Ready - finished

4 servings - time required: 30 minutes

Garlic-Lemon Rice

Ingredients
225g rice

2 tbsp parsley, chopped

2 tbsp. vegan butter

Lemon peel, ground

1 clove of garlic

360ml vegetable stock

1 pinch of salt

Nutrient information per serving
226 Calories
7g Fat
38g Carbohydrates
3g Protein

- Add rice, vegetable stock, salt and garlic clove to the rice pan and mix well.
- Cooking.
- Once cooked, remove the clove of garlic.
- Mix rice with the fork and add the remaining ingredients.
- Stir well and leave in the rice cooker for another ten minutes.
- Serve warm and enjoy.

4 servings - time required: 40 minutes

Coriander rice

Ingredients
225g white rice

2.5g ground cilantro

360ml water

Half an onion, diced

1 tablespoon olive oil

1 pinch of salt

Nutrient information per serving
203 Calories
3g Fat
37g Carbohydrates
3g Protein

- Select "Brown rice" setting.
- Heat the olive oil in a rice cooker.
- When the oil is hot, add the onion and fry.
- Add the remaining ingredients and mix well.
- Select the "White rice" setting and cook the ingredients.
- After cooking, let it rest for 15 minutes in the holding mode.
- Mix the rice with the fork and serve.

2 servings - time required: 30 minutes

Coriander-Lemon Rice

Ingredients
225g white rice

3 tbsp. coriander, chopped up

Half a juice of a squeezed lemon

2 tablespoons olive oil

500ml water

1 pinch of salt

- Add salt, rice, water and olive oil to the rice and stir well.
- Close the lid and cook with the "White rice" setting.
- When the cooking is done, add the coriander and lemon juice. Mix everything well.
- Serve, enjoy.

Nutrient information per serving
378 Calories
5g Fat
74g Carbohydrates
6g Protein

4 servings - time required: 50 minutes

Mushroom rice with cabbage and green beans

Ingredients
450g rice
3 finely chopped spring onions
1-2 tablespoons rice wine
3 tablespoons soy sauce
8 edible mushrooms, crushed
10 green beans, crushed
Half an onion, chopped
One quarter cabbage head, crushed
1 peeled and sliced carrot
500ml water
Half a teaspoon of salt

Nutrient information per serving
417 Calories
1g Fat
91g Carbohydrates
11g Protein

- Add rice, water, salt, rice wine and soy sauce in a rice cooker.
- Place the remaining ingredients on top. DO NOT stir.
- Close the lid and boil the contents.
- After cooking, mix well and serve.

2 servings - time required: 1 hour 20 minutes

Salmon potato gratin

Ingredients
4 large potatoes, thin slices

2 wild salmon fillets

250ml milk

1 egg

2 tbsp/30g butter

1 pinch of salt

1 pinch of pepper

Nutrient information per serving
348 Calories
15g Fat
25g Carbohydrates
26g Protein

- Put butter in the rice cooker.
- Lay out the cooker with potato slices.
- Spread a quarter of the salmon over the potatoes.
- Sprinkle with salt and pepper.
- Next layer of potato salmon until everything is in the cooker.
- Mix milk and egg in a bowl. about the potatoes.
- Cook for 60 minutes.

2 servings - time required: 12-24 hours or 30 minutes working time

Prepare tasty corn dip

Ingredients
4 Corn cobs
40g bacon cubes, browned (alternative: bacon slices)
500ml sour cream
240g cow's milk cheese
120g diced peppers
120g Jalapeno, diced
75g spring onions, thin sliced
1 pinch of salt and pepper

Nutrient information per serving
132 Calories
2g Fat
34g Carbohydrates
11g Protein

- Add 500ml water in a rice kettle.
- Heat until it boils.
- Add the corn on the cobs and steam.
- Add the remaining ingredients, mix well and leave to rest in the refrigerator overnight.
- Done.

3 servings - 35 minutes

Tasty Basmati rice

Ingredients
225g Basmati rice

3 cardamom capsules or alternatively a knife point of ground cardamom

1 stick of cinnamon

37.5ml water

1 pinch of salt

Nutrient information per serving
265 Calories
2g Fat
54g Carbohydrates
5g Protein

- Add the ingredients to the rice and mix well.
- Cook with "White rice" setting.
- After cooking, let it rest for 15 minutes with the warming function.
- Stir the rice well with the fork and remove the cinnamon stick.
- Optional if applicable: Remove cardamom capsules.
- Serve and enjoy.

4 servings - time required: 20 minutes

Delicious coconut rice

Ingredients

225g white rice

15g ground coconut

Half a teaspoon of mustard seeds

250ml water

1 pinch of cardamom, ground

Half a teaspoon of salt

- Add the ingredients to the rice and mix well.
- Close the rice cooker lid and allow the contents to boil.
- Wait 10 minutes as soon as the rice cooker is ready and has switched to the warming function.
- Mix well and serve.

Nutrient information per serving
207 Calories
2g Fat
42g Carbohydrates
4g Protein

4 servings - time required: 30 minutes

Delicious Mexican rice

Ingredients
225g rice
120g green peppers, hot and crushed
2 cloves of garlic, chopped
45g peppers, chopped
75g onions, diced
2 tablespoons olive oil
90g tomato paste
500ml vegetable stock

Nutrient information per serving
368 Calories
9g Fat
63g Carbohydrates
10g Protein

- Put all the ingredients in a rice cooker and mix well.
- Boil until either all the water has been absorbed or the rice is through.
- Stir well and enjoy.

4 servings - time required: 35 minutes

Tasty risotto

Ingredients
225g arborio rice

60ml dry white wine

120g onions, minced

1 tablespoon olive oil

1 dash of saffron

750ml vegetable stock

Nutrient information per serving
255 Calories
4g Fat
40g Carbohydrates
3g Protein

- Heat saffron and vegetable stock in a pan and leave to stand for 10 minutes.
- In the meantime, start the cooker with the fast cooking function.
- Add olive oil and onion and cook for two minutes.
- Add the remaining ingredients and mix well.
- Close the lid and cook for 20 minutes.
- Finally, stir well and serve.

10 servings - time required: 1 hour 10 minutes

Tomato Beans Quinoa

Ingredients
360g Quinoa

60g taco spice

240ml water

300g oz tomatoes, diced

450g black beans, soak overnight and wash before cooking

Nutrient information per serving
288 Calories
3g Fat
50g Carbohydrates
14g Protein

- Add the ingredients to the rice and stir well.
- Select the brown rice setting and let the quinoa mixture cook for one hour.
- Stir and serve the ready-made mixture.

4 servings - time required: 30 minutes

Lenses Quinoa

Ingredients
255g Quinoa, washed and dried

1,2l water

100g Green lentils

A quarter bunch of basil

1 pinch of chili powder

1 tsp paprika or pepper powder

- Add the ingredients to the rice and mix well.
- Cook for 20 minutes with the white rice setting.
- Again stir well and serve.

Nutrient information per serving
322 Calories
4g Fat
55g Carbohydrates
15g Protein

2 servings - time required: 30 minutes

Corn cabbage Quinoa

Ingredients
43g Quinoa, washed and dried

140g green cabbage

90g corn

120ml water

A touch of pepper

A pinch of salt

Nutrient information per serving
144 Calories
2g Fat
27g Carbohydrates
6g Protein

- Add water, quinoa and corn to the rice cooker and mix well.
- Place the kale on the steamed cooking surface over the quinoa.
- Cook for 20 minutes.
- After cooking, mix the cabbage and quinoa in a bowl.
- Season to taste with salt and pepper.
- Enjoy!

5 servings - time required: 30 minutes

Corn-Olive-Carrot-Pea Quinoa

Ingredients
170g Quinoa, washed and dried
120ml water
240g carrots, finely chopped
240g peas
180g Black olives, halved
420g sweet corn
450ml vegetable stock
2 tbsp. tomato paste

Nutrient information per serving
608 Calories
11g Fat
117g Carbohydrates
23g Protein

- Put the quinoa, water, vegetable stock and tomato paste in a rice kettle.
- Switch on the device.
- Heat the remaining vegetables in the microwave for two minutes.
- Once the quinoa mixture is cooked, add the remaining vegetables. Mix well.
- Serve warm and enjoy.

4 servings - time required: 45 minutes

Sea rice magic

Ingredients
15 shrimp, peeled and spilled
Squid pieces, washed and diced, quantity according to preference (3 pieces recommended)
450g rice
750ml water
2 star aniseed
3 sticks of cinnamon
3 cloves
3 tbsp raisins
2cm turmeric, ground
1 garlic clove, ground
2 kaffir lime, halved
3 tbsp. cooking oil
Cashew nuts - according to your own taste

Nutrient information per serving
312 Calories
8g Fat
31g Carbohydrates
25g Protein

- Heat the oil. Sauté turmeric, cloves, garlic, cinnamon sticks and star aniseed.
- Put all the ingredients in the rice cooker together with the rice and the remaining ingredients. Mix well.
- Fill in enough water that the mixture is completely covered with water.
- After cooking garnish with cashew nuts.
- Serving.

2 servings - time expenditure: 40 minutes

Midnight omelette

Ingredients
Half a spring onion, thinly sliced
2 tbsp coriander, ground
200g vegetables of your choice
1 teaspoon butter
1 handful of cultivated mushrooms
3 eggs
1 tablespoon coffee cream
50g Cheddar, grated
1 pinch of salt
1 pinch of pepper

Nutrient information per serving
475 Calories
38g Fat
4g Carbohydrates
28g Protein

- Preheat for 10 minutes with the lid closed. Use the steam cooking function for this.
- Add butter and mushrooms. The same goes for spring onions, coriander, vegetables and tomatoes. Sauté for two minutes.
- Whisk beaten eggs, salt, coffee cream and pepper in a bowl.
- Pour carefully over the vegetables in the rice cooker and mix.
- Close the lid and cook for 12-14 minutes.
- Garnish with the cheese and mix the mixture.
- Done.

2 servings - time required: 45 minutes

Delicious mussel mix

Ingredients
30g butter
150g diced onions
100g celery, chopped
2 cloves of garlic, ground
225g potatoes, diced
10g flour
500ml vegetable stock
200ml cream (approx. 1 cup)
300g mussels
1 bay leaf
1 sprig of thyme

Nutrient information per serving
423 Calories
12g Fat
32g Carbohydrates
24g Protein

- Sauté the onions, garlic and celery in the rice cooker for 5 minutes.
- Add flour and mix well.
- Add vegetable stock and bay leaf.
- Add thyme and potatoes. Mix well.
- Let it simmer for 20 minutes.
- Add fish stock, mussels and whipped cream. Mix well.
- Cook for 10 minutes.
- Done.

Time required: 25 minutes

Orange marmalade

Ingredients
500g unpeeled oranges

250g sugar

Nutrient information per serving
49 Calories
0g Fat
13g Carbohydrates
0g Protein

- Cut orange into small pieces. Remove the white core.
- Optional: Remove orange peel.
- Add oranges and sugar to the rice cooker.
- Sauté for 15 minutes.
- Place the jam in sterile glass. Close tightly.
- Done.

3 servings - time required: 35 minutes

Orange-Rice Plov

Ingredients
250g rice

2 tbsp. 30g butter, unsalted

40g diced onions, diced

juice of 2 pressed oranges

450ml chicken stock

1 pinch of salt

40g roasted almonds

Nutrient information per serving
179 Calories
5g Fat
28g Carbohydrates
4g Protein

- Put all the ingredients (except the almonds) in the rice cooker. Cook for 20 minutes.
- Allow to rest for 10 minutes.
- Garnish with almonds.
- Enjoy.

2 servings - time expenditure: 40 minutes

Pancetta with green cabbage and spaghetti pumpkin

Ingredients
Half a spaghetti pumpkin, pitted
2 cloves of garlic
120g Pancetta
1 onion, diced
140g cabbage, chopped and debarked
25g Parmesan cheese, grated

Nutrient information per serving
265 Calories
7g Fat
17g Carbohydrates
9g Protein

- Put half a pumpkin with water in the rice cooker.
- Steam cooked for 20 minutes.
- Remove the pumpkin and put it aside.
- fry onions, pancetta and garlic for 10 minutes
- Add cabbage and cheese and fry for another 3 minutes.
- Remove the pumpkin threads. Mix the remaining pumpkin with the cooked mixture. Cut into small pieces as a filling or pumpkin and mix in a mixing bowl.
- Done.

6 servings - 35 minutes

Pasta Carbonara

Ingredients
2l water
6 slices of bacon
75g onions, diced
1 clove of garlic
1 egg
2-3 cups of whipped cream
400g pasta
100g Parmesan cheese, grated
2 teaspoons salt
1 pinch of pepper

Nutrient information per serving
307 Calories
7g Fat
45g Carbohydrates
19g Protein

- Select "Brown rice" setting.
- Fry the garlic, onions and bacon. Then set aside.
- Put water in rice kettle. Set to steam and cook for 7 minutes.
- Put the pasta into the rice cooker and cook.
- Drain the pasta and place it in the rice cooker (now switched off).
- Mix the remaining ingredients in a bowl.
- Add to the rice cooker and mix with the pasta.
- Add the fried mixture of bacon and cook for another 5 minutes.
- Done.

4 servings - time required: 4 hours or 50 minutes working time

Peppermint truffle

Ingredients
240g dark chocolate

60ml whipped cream

1 teaspoon peppermint extract

240g Candy canes, crushed

250ml water

Nutrient information per serving
210 Calories
14g Fat
19g Carbohydrates
2g Protein

- Put water into the rice cooker.
- Place the glass bowl in the rice cooker. Pour chocolate and whipped cream into them.
- Place the rice cooker on steam and stir the mixture while heating.
- Once the chocolate has melted, add the peppermint extract.
- Allow the glass bowl and its contents to cool in the refrigerator for at least one hour.
- Leave to rest for another 2 hours at room temperature.
- Form small meatballs-sized truffles from the chocolate dough.
- Place the chopped sugar stick pieces on a plate and coat the shaped truffles with it by rolling them over.
- Done.

6 servings - time required: 40 minutes

Mushroom rice Plov

Ingredients

340g white rice

2 tsp ground garlic

2 teaspoons olive oil

Half an onion, chopped

75g mushroom, sliced

35g almond slivers

500ml vegetable stock

Nutrient information per serving
224 Calories
4g Fat
39g Carbohydrates
6g Protein

- Heat olive oil in a saucepan at medium heat.
- Add the onions and garlic and fry.
- Put the contents of the pot and the remaining ingredients in a rice cooker and mix well.
- Close the lid and let it boil.
- Mix again and serve.

3 persons - time expenditure: 12 hours or 35 minutes working time

Pinto beans rice cooker type

Ingredients
400g pint beans

1,5l water

2 tbsp. salt

- Rinse the beans and soak them overnight.
- Dry the beans and add water and salt to the rice kettle.
- Cook with "White rice" setting.
- Done.

Nutrient information per serving
245 Calories
1g Fat
44g Carbohydrates
15g Protein

1 serving - 45 minutes

Polenta with cheese

Ingredients
30g butter
Half an onion, diced
1 clove of garlic, minced
250ml chicken stock
250ml milk
80g polenta
1 pinch of salt
60g cheddar, grated
60g Parmesan cheese, grated
1 pinch of pepper

Nutrient information per serving
295 Calories
7g Fat
26g Carbohydrates
33g Protein

- Add butter, garlic and onions to the rice pan.
- Close the lid and cook for 10-15 minutes.
- Add chicken stock, polenta, milk and salt. Mix well, close the lid and cook for another 20 minutes.
- Add cheese and pepper. Switch on the warm-keeping function. Stir continuously until the cheese is melted and well distributed.
- Serving

2 servings - time expenditure: 40 minutes

Quiche from the rice cooker

Ingredients
4 eggs
1 cup whipped cream
50g cheese, grated
120g Pancetta, sliced
75g onions, diced
200g cabbage, chopped
1 pinch of pepper
100g bread

Nutrient information per serving
362 Calories
8g Fat
30g Carbohydrates
19g Protein

- Sauté the onions, cabbage and pancetta. As soon as it is ready, lay separately to the side.
- Put the bread in a rice cooker.
- Mix the eggs, cheese and whipped cream with the fried meat.
- Add the mixture prepared in this way to the bread and season with pepper.
- Select "White rice" setting and cook.
- Done.

4 servings - time required: 30 minutes

Quinoa broccoli casserole

Ingredients
250g Quinoa, washed and dried
2 teaspoons of lime juice
1 tablespoon of vegetarian butter
4 cloves of garlic, chopped
1 broccoli head
30g vegetarian cheese
750ml water
pepper
salt

Nutrient information per serving
290 Calories
8g Fat
44g Carbohydrates
10g Protein

- Put butter in rice cooker and sweat
- When the butter is liquid, add the garlic and stir for 30 seconds.
- Add Quinoa and mix well.
- Add water and lime juice and close the lid.
- As soon as half of the liquid has been absorbed, open the lid and mix.
- Spread the crushed broccoli over the quinoa and close the lid again.
- Once the broccoli is well cooked, open the lid and add cheese. Stir well until the cheese is completely melted.
- Serve and enjoy.

4 servings - time required: 30 minutes

Quinoa vegetables Plov

Ingredients
120g Quinoa, 15min soaked and dried
420ml vegetable stock
100g peppers, chopped
Half a teaspoon of turmeric
75g mushrooms, chopped
115 celery, chopped
25g carrots
75g onions, chopped
1 clove of garlic, chopped
1 tablespoon olive oil

Nutrient information per serving
277 Calories
6g Fat
32g Carbohydrates
9g Protein

- Heat olive oil in a pan at medium heat.
- Add the onion, garlic, mushrooms, celery and carrots in a saucepan and sauté for 4 minutes.
- Add turmeric root and quinoa and sweat for 2 minutes.
- Put the contents of the pot in a rice cooker.
- Add vegetable stock and chopped peppers and mix well.
- Cook with white rice setting.
- Mix well and serve.

1 serving - time required: 25 minutes

Quinoa with juicy apple

Ingredients
43g Quinoa, washed and dried

60ml water

1 teaspoon cinnamon

2 tsp lime juice

1 apple, seeded and cut

- Mix apple, cinnamon, water and lime juice in a mixer.
- Add the ready-made apple mixture and quinoa to the rice cooker. Stir well as usual.
- Boil until the water is completely absorbed.
- Finally, stir again and serve.

Nutrient information per serving
280 Calories
3g Fat
60g Carbohydrates
6g Protein

2 servings - time required: 15 minutes

Smoked salmon fritatta

Ingredients
6 eggs

120g smoked salmon

1 tbsp. /15g butter

2 tbsp coriander, ground

1 pinch of pepper

- Whisk eggs and pepper in a bowl.
- Brush the base of the cooker with butter. Pour the whisked mixture into the rice cooker. Salmon and spices are on top.
- Close the lid and cook for five minutes.
- Finished.

Nutrient information per serving
232 Calories
3g Fat
9g Carbohydrates
8g Protein

2 servings - time required: 25 minutes

Brussel sprouts with walnut oil

Ingredients
120ml water
500g Brussels sprouts, halved
70g ground almonds
1 clove of garlic
60g Cranberries, ground
1 tbsp Agavensyrup
1 tablespoon walnut oil
1 tablespoon olive oil
1 pinch of salt and pepper

Nutrient information per serving
163 Calories
6g Fat
19g Carbohydrates
11g Protein

- Sauté Brussels sprouts in a rice cooker with olive oil for 5 minutes.
- Add spring onions and garlic. Sauté for 3-4 more minutes.
- Add the cranberries, water and agave. Continue cooking for 5 minutes.
- Add the remaining ingredients and mix well.
- Serving.

1-4 servings - time: 1 hour

Rosemary chicken

Ingredients

500-1500g chicken (depending on the portion quantity)

2 onions, peeled

1 lemon

2 rosemary branches

30g butter

1 pinch of salt and pepper

Nutrient information per serving
224 Calories
4g Fat
21g Carbohydrates
26g Protein

- Cut the onions into halves and place them in the rice cooker with the flat side facing down.
- Halve the lemon in half and put it with rosemary into the chicken.
- Rub chicken with butter and season to taste with salt and pepper.
- Place the chicken on top of the rice cooker on the onions.
- Cook with "White rice" setting. After cooking, check that it is ready. If not: allow the chicken another cooking pass.
- Done.

4 servings - time required: 30 minutes

Red Quinoa with rice

Ingredients

85g red Quinoa, rinsed and dried

750ml water

225g ready-to-cook rice

1 tablespoon olive oil

A pinch of salt

- Add the ingredients to the rice and mix well.
- Cooking.
- As soon as the rice cooker changes to keep warm, open the lid.
- Mix and serve the prepared dish well.

Nutrient information per serving
284 Calories
4g Fat
54g Carbohydrates
5g Protein

2 servings - time required: 25 minutes

San Antonio rice

Ingredients
190g rice
1 tin/100ml salsa sauce
1 tablespoon vegetable oil
1 tin of corn
Half a teaspoon of caraway seeds
1 pinch of salt
1 pinch of pepper
300ml water
coriander

- Add all ingredients except coriander to the rice cooker. Mix well and cook with the setting "White rice".
- Allow to cool for 8-10 minutes. Now garnish with coriander (quantity according to personal taste).
- Done.

Nutrient information per serving
189 Calories
3g Fat
30g Carbohydrates
10g Protein

Time required: 30 minutes

Hot cheese dip

Ingredients
1 onion, diced

1 jalapeno, diced

1 tomato, diced

1 teaspoon olive oil

0,2l Pils

360g Spiced semi-hard cheese

120g White Cheddar

Nutrient information per serving
80 Calories
6g Fat
5g Carbohydrates
1g Protein

- Put the rice cooker on a sautéed dish and add the lump of oil.
- Sauté the jalapeno, onions and tomatoes in it.
- Add 50ml of beer and boil the mixture until all liquid has evaporated.
- Add the cheese and the remaining beer and stir well until all the liquid is absorbed or evaporated.
- Done.

6 servings - time required: 50 minutes

Sharp lentil rice

Ingredients
150g lentils
340g Brown Rice
1 pinch of parsley
1 pinch of cumin seed
6 cloves
1l water
2 sticks of cinnamon
2 tbsp. lime juice
1 pinch of pepper
1 teaspoon salt

Nutrient information per serving
297 Calories
3g Fat
55g Carbohydrates
10g Protein

- Add all the ingredients except the lime juice and the parsley to the rice kettle and mix well.
- Let it boil until either the water is completely absorbed or the rice and the lentils are soft boiled.
- Then add cloves and cinnamon.
- Add lime juice and parsley and mix well.
- Serve warm.

2 servings - time expenditure: 40 minutes

Fast rice cooker paste

Ingredients
200g noodles

360ml chicken stock

1 teaspoon salt

250ml milk

150g cheese, grated

- Put the pasta, chicken broth and salt in the rice cooker and cook for 15 minutes.
- Then add the cheese and milk. Cook for another 20 minutes.
- Optional: Add finely chopped broccoli.
- After cooking, mix well and serve.

Nutrient information per serving
260 Calories
7g Fat
36g Carbohydrates
12g Protein

2 servings - time required: 25 minutes

Fast chicken curry

Ingredients
2 tbsp. cooking oil
150g diced onions
1 clove of garlic, minced
2 tbsp curry powder
500ml water
1 tin of tomatoes, strained
450g chicken breast, shredded
75g raisins
190g natural yoghurt
50g cashew nuts
250g rice mixture

Nutrient information per serving
268 Calories
6g Fat
27g Carbohydrates
23g Protein

- Heat the oil in the rice cooker.
- Add garlic and onions. Allow the mixture to cook for five minutes.
- Add curry powder. Cook for another two minutes.
- Add the rest and mix well.
- Let it boil with normal settings.
- Serving.

2 servings - time required: 20 minutes

Fast Quinoa-Porridge

Ingredients
85g Quinoa, rinsed and dried

250ml water

35g almonds

1 apple, sliced

250ml almond milk

50g oatmeal

1 tablespoon maple syrup

Nutrient information per serving
663 Calories
38g Fat
72g Carbohydrates
14g Protein

- Put the quinoa, oats, almond milk and water in a rice kettle and mix well.
- Cook the mixture in the closed cooker for 15 minutes.
- Mix well after 15 minutes.
- Add the quinoa mixture in a bowl and add chopped almonds, apple slices and maple syrup.
- Serve warm and enjoy.

4 servings - time required: 2 hours

Swiss rice cake

Ingredients
120g long grain rice
200g sugar
1 pinch of salt
1 tablespoon butter, unsalted
750ml milk
Lemon zest
70g ground almonds
1 tbsp flour
3 beaten eggs

Pie-Crust:
190g flour
Half a teaspoon of salt
2 tablespoons sugar
115g butter
4 tbsp water

Nutrient information per serving
307 Calories
7g Fat
45g Carbohydrates
19g Protein

- Cook rice in the rice cooker as usual.
- Put the milk, butter, sugar and salt together with the finished rice in a pan and bring to the boil at medium heat.
- As soon as it boils, turn the stove down and let it simmer for another 25 minutes.
- Allow to cool and then puree.
- Pour the mixture into a bowl with lemon zest, almonds, pie-crust and flour. Stir in the eggs.
- Cook in a rice cooker with the "white rice" setting.
- Finished.
- To make the pie-crust, mix flour, salt and sugar in a bowl. Add butter in small pieces and knead. Pour cold water over the dough and form a large ball. Then roll out the dough and put it in a baking tin for one hour in the refrigerator.

Time required: 4 days - Working time: 30 minutes

Prepare homemade kimchi

Ingredients
1 Chinese cabbage, chopped
1 winter radish, sliced
6 Bird Eye Chilis, chopped
2 cloves of garlic, ground
75g spring onions, diced
2 tablespoons ginger powder
1 pinch of salt
2 tbsp. rice vinegar
1 teaspoon sugar

Nutrient information per serving
154 Calories
2g Fat
15g Carbohydrates
9g Protein

- Fill the pot with 500ml water. Add a little salt.
- Add cabbage and stir.
- Leave the pot with the lid to stand for 24 hours. Open briefly once in a while and stir again.
- Skim off the excess water after 24 hours.
- Add the remaining ingredients.
- Seal well and close tightly.
- Let it rest for three days.
- Durable kimchi as an ingredient for your rice dishes is ready.

4 servings - time required: 35 minutes

Shrimps with Grits

Ingredients
500g shrimps, peeled and elbowed
Half an onion, diced
1 garlic clove, ground
50g butter
2 slices of bacon, finely chopped
170g Grits
100g Parmesan cheese
1 pinch of salt
1 pinch of pepper

Nutrient information per serving
296 Calories
6g Fat
30g Carbohydrates
27g Protein

- Heat the water in the rice cooker with the steam gas setting.
- When the water boils, add the grit, stir and continue to boil for 5 minutes.
- Add butter and cheese. Mix thoroughly and allow the mixture to cool.
- Sauté the bacon in a pan.
- Add onions and garlic and fry.
- Add shrimps and pour beer over it. Fry it.
- Season to taste with salt and pepper.
- Pour the contents of the pan with the shrimps over the finished grit.
- Done.

3 servings - time expenditure: 50 minutes

Shrimps with lemon risotto

Ingredients
2 tablespoons extra virgin olive oil
2 tbsp/30g butter
150g diced onions
1 tbsp. lemon peel, ground
225g rice
60ml white wine
750ml chicken stock
12 shrimps, peeled and spiked
175g corn kernels
3 tablespoons lemon juice
50g Parmesan cheese
1 pinch of pepper
1 bunch of parsley, chopped
4 lemon wedges
1 pinch of salt

Nutrient information per serving
434 Calories
11g Fat
47g Carbohydrates
31g Protein

- Select the quick cooking function.
- Add oil and a tablespoon of butter. Sauté the onions in the mixture for three minutes. Add the lemon wedges and mix well.
- Add the rice, mix thoroughly and simmer for four minutes.
- Add the wine and simmer for 4 minutes.
- Add the vegetable stock and mix.
- Cook for 20 minutes.
- Stir in shrimps with lemon juice and corn. Cook for 5 minutes.
- Add the remaining butter and mix well.
- Add salt, pepper and then top with parmesan cheese.

1-2 servings - time required: 25 minutes

Asparagus with tofu

Ingredients
Half a bunch of asparagus
200g tofu, chopped
Half a carrot, cut and peeled
1 garlic clove, ground
Optional: 2 tablespoons oyster sauce
1 tablespoon soy sauce
1 teaspoon vegetable oil
1 teaspoon sesame oil
1 teaspoon of rice wine
1 teaspoon honey

Nutrient information per serving
174 Calories
5g Fat
22g Carbohydrates
13g Protein

- Pour ingredients into a bowl and mix well.
- Place in the steam oven.
- Steam cooked for 20 minutes.
- Serving.

5 servings - time required: 1 hour 10 minutes

Spinach, chickpea and green cabbage Quinoa

Ingredients
170g Quinoa, washed and dried
500ml water
6 tbsp. lime juice
3 tablespoons olive oil
120g dried cranberries
200g chickpeas, soaked and dried overnight
350 g spinach, minced
130g green cabbage, chopped

- Add the ingredients in a rice cooker and mix.
- Cooking.
- Stir well twice during cooking.
- After cooking, stir again and serve.

Nutrient information per serving
371 Calories
13g Fat
50g Carbohydrates
13g Protein

2 servings - time: 1 hour

Southern corn pudding

Ingredients
500ml water

30-300g cream corn

500ml milk, low-fat

2 eggs

3 tablespoons sugar

1 pinch of salt

2 tbsp flour

1 tbsp. 15g butter

Nutrient information per serving
323 Calories
8g Fat
21g Carbohydrates
11g Protein

- Put water into the rice cooker.
- Bring to the boil. It takes about 8 minutes.
- In a bowl, add milk, corn, sugar, eggs, flour and salt and mix.
- Pour the dough into the rice cooker. Spread with butter.
- Cover with aluminium foil and cook for 45 minutes.

4 servings - time required: 35 minutes

Sweet potatoes with rice

Ingredients
450g rice

500ml water

1 sweet potato, peeled and cut

1 pinch of salt

- Mix the ingredients in the rice cooker well.
- Cooking.
- Mix the rice with a fork and serve.

Nutrient information per serving
363 Calories
1g Fat
79g Carbohydrates
7g Protein

4 servings - time required: 30 minutes

Sweet pudding

Ingredients
400g white rice
25g pistachios, crushed
30g dried cherries
2 tsp. cardamom
150g coconut blossom sugar
500ml rice milk
450ml coconut milk

- Add the ingredients to the rice cooker and mix well.
- Cooking with the "White rice" setting.
- Finally, stir again and serve.

Nutrient information per serving
700 Calories
28g Fat
104g Carbohydrates
9g Protein

3 servings - time required: 30 minutes

Thai rice

Ingredients
225g Jasmine rice

500ml coconut milk

1 pinch of cardamom

Half a teaspoon of coriander

1 pinch of salt

Nutrient information per serving
237 Calories
4g Fat
31g Carbohydrates
10g Protein

- Put all the ingredients in a rice cooker and cook with the "white rice" setting.
- Leave to rest for 10 minutes after cooking.
- Serve and enjoy.

2 servings - time expenditure: 40 minutes

Vegetarian noodle soup

Ingredients
1 tablespoon olive oil
1 garlic clove, ground
1 onion, diced
3 carrots, cut and peeled
400g peas
450g strained tomatoes
150ml vegetable juice
60ml water
3 tablespoons red wine
2 tbsp Worcestershiresauce
200g Farfallen noodles
1 pinch of spice mixture
1 pinch of salt and pepper

Nutrient information per serving
321 Calories
6g Fat
41g Carbohydrates
12g Protein

- Preheat for 10 minutes with the steam cooking function.
- Add the oil, onions and garlic. Fry it.
- Add the remaining ingredients.
- Cook for 25 minutes.
- Serving.

6 servings - time required: 40 minutes

Vegetarian Curried Rice

Ingredients
450g white rice
50 carrots, diced
225g potatoes, diced
250g diced tofu
4 bay leaves
3 tbsp lemongrass
1 tablespoon olive oil
3 tbsp curry powder
500ml water

- Add the ingredients to the rice cooker and mix.
- Cook for 30 minutes.
- Mix and serve in a bowl.

Nutrient information per serving
304 Calories
5g Fat
56g Carbohydrates
8g Protein

6 servings - time required: 1 hour 10 minutes

Vegetarian Black Bean-Chili

Ingredients
1 tablespoon olive oil
2 peeled and sliced carrots
Half an onion, diced
2 ground garlic cloves
2 tbsp. chili powder
1 tablespoon cumin seed
900g Black Bean, washed and dried
450g Black Beans, with liquid
230g bean purée

Nutrient information per serving
417 Calories
5g Fat
22g Carbohydrates
27g Protein

- Sauté the onion with oil in a frying pan over medium heat.
- Add carrots and garlic. Sauté until the onions are nice brown.
- Put the fried mixture with vegetable stock, cumin, tomatoes and chili powder in a rice cooker. Cook for 20 minutes with the pressure cooker.
- Add the black beans and cook for a further 20 minutes with the pressure cooker.
- Add the bean puree and mix well.
- Garnish with cheese and avocado.
- Serving.

4-6 servings - time required: 30 minutes

Wheat sprout salad

Ingredients
450g rice

500ml water

1 pinch of salt

180g wheat sprouts

- Sauté the sprouts in a pan for 4 minutes.
- Cook with rice and salt in a rice cooker.

Nutrient information per serving
132 Calories
2g Fat
34g Carbohydrates
11g Protein

3 servings - time required: 30 minutes

Lemon Dill Rice

Ingredients
225g rice
450ml water
1 pinch of salt
1 lemon zest
1 tablespoon lemon juice
1 tsp dill, dried
Parsley (quantity according to personal taste)
2 tbsp/30g butter
1 pinch of salt and pepper

Nutrient information per serving
307 Calories
7g Fat
45g Carbohydrates
19g Protein

- Put ingredients in a rice cooker and cook with the "white rice" setting.
- Allow to rest for 10 minutes.
- Serve and enjoy.

4 servings - time required: 30 minutes

Lemongrass shrimp soup

Ingredients
500g shrimps, discovered and washed
2 carrots, sliced
2 celery sticks, chopped
Half an onion, diced
2 cloves of garlic, chopped
2 thin slices of ginger tuber
2 tbsp Pul beaver ("leafy pepper")
1 lemongrass
1l vegetable stock
2 tablespoons coconut oil

Nutrient information per serving
65 Calories
5g Fat
7g Carbohydrates
9g Protein

- Finely chop the lemongrass and add. Cut off brown spots and stems.
- Put on sauté and add oil. The same goes for vegetables, ginger and garlic. Sauté for 10 minutes.
- Add vegetable stock and Pul beaver. Cook for 10 minutes.
- Add shrimps and cook for another 2 minutes.
- Done.

Imprint

Mattis Lundqvist
Represented by: Christina Sorg c/o Papyrus Authors Club
R. O. M. Logicware GmbH
Pettenkoferstr. 16-18
10247 Berlin
Images: depositphotos. com; @ etorres69; @ photominer; @ Anna_Shepulova; @ olhaafansieva; @ coolfonk; @denio109; @lenyvavsha @ belchonock

Printing house: Amazon Media EU S. à. r. l.
5 Rue Plaetis
L-2338 Luxembourg

Printed in Great Britain
by Amazon